From Fear to Freedom

Peter Black

Published in Australia by Shining Bright
Publishing
Second Edition 2013

ISBN: 978-1493630929

Cover Photo: Lana Morgan
Flinders Reef, Queensland, Australia - Cape
Moreton is in the background

Contents

Acknowledgements

Jonathan G of the cult information service.

I would like to acknowledge and thank Jonathan for helping me personalize my story from the start and also must thank him for putting many hours of his time into proof-reading and editing. As well as this, he has been essential in placing this book on the net, enabling me to "get it out there".

Les Barkla.

Acknowledgement and thanks also goes to my cousin Les for his assistance with proof reading and for his strong encouragement and belief as I wrote this story.

Joan Black.

This lady and I met and married in the former cult. We suffered some very tough times together as a result of our cultic lives and are no longer a couple. A friendship remains and I wish to acknowledge Joan for her permission to mention her in this story. Also for encouragement during the writing of it.

Colin and Gladys Black.

Acknowledgement is given to my parents for encouragement as I wrote the story and I also wish to praise them as they are healing from the damage caused by their own membership in the Worldwide Church of God.

Ron Ion.

Ron has been a mate of mine for about 30 years or more and also spent 5 years at a college run by the cult in the US. As such, he was able to tell me about the sect as it was outside Australia.

ACKNOWLEDGEMENTS

Hazel Carter.

During our relationship many years after I left the cult, Hazel expressed a lot of interest in my life in it and I wish to acknowledge her for the idea of writing this book in the first place.

Renate Koehn and Ros Fraser.

These very close and dear friends believe strongly in the healing I am attempting to bring about by the writing of this story and I acknowledge and thank them for that.

My neighbours:

As a group, I want to gratefully acknowledge my wonderful neighbours and friends in Thorneside Queensland where I live for their belief in this book and also for much encouragement as I wrote it.

FROM FEAR TO FREEDOM

Introduction

In Australia and many other similar countries around the world such as the US, UK, Canada and New Zealand just to name a few, we value highly our individual right to make choices. These start in childhood when we may decide which sports we would like to play and later in secondary school, we may also decide which subjects we wish to concentrate on. We do this in order to prepare for employment or for a place at college or university. As adults, we choose where we want to live, where we would like to go for holidays and when an election is called which political party will attract our vote. We call such rights which we enjoy, freedom and we say that we live in a "free country".

In some countries though, such freedom of choice and individual decision making is not permitted. Many aspects of daily life are monitored and controlled by repressive and authoritarian governments.

FROM FEAR TO FREEDOM

Unfortunately even in nations like ours, organizations and groups exist which reduce or eliminate the freedom of their members in order to control them.

If such groups have a religious or political basis we call them cults and they still flourish even in these "enlightened times". Australia allows freedom of religion and cults or sects which abuse this right have existed for many years and will continue to crop up from time to time.

Because cults bring about fear and low self-esteem in their members not to mention how they damage the ability of people who later leave to trust, they cause enormous disruption to lives.

Cults may exist supposedly under the banner of any of the major religions of the world however it is the effect of the so-called Christian or bible-based groups which will be examined here. It is my intention to help the reader to identify harmful cults in order to avoid becoming mixed-up in one to begin with.

Also it is a goal of this book to lend as much assistance as possible to people who are intending to leave such a cult or who are trying to rebuild their lives after having done so. Chapter 9, *Helping The Helper*, assists anyone who is trying to help a relative or friend to rebuild their life after breaking away from such a controlling group.

This material isn't meant to be a brag-fest about how I have rebuilt my life after my own time in a cult however I will use large amounts of my story along with research to assist other cult survivors as much as possible.

It should be a reason to celebrate when you or someone you know breaks away from a cult but sometimes a person in that position cannot handle the sudden freedom. This can lead to returning to the sect from which he or she came, getting mixed-up in another cult, going onto alcohol or drugs in an effort to cope with life and tragically, even to suicide. Therefore it is important to get it right as lives may depend on it.

I spent 31 years in a formerly large cult with members in most countries of the world. It was called the Worldwide Church of God (WCG) or often just called Worldwide by former members. This group was started by its founder Herbert W. Armstrong on the US west coast in the state of Oregon.

After leaving the sect, I faced the demanding and hugely difficult challenge of trying to rebuild my life. I did some things right and some things wrong while trying to do so. The worst mistake I made was firstly not to recognize just how much damage had been done to my ability to think normally by the controlling sect.

Secondly, I didn't seek help from anyone to put my life back together for many years and I hope to help readers of this material to avoid making those same errors.

Chapter 1: The Worldwide Church of God

Herbert W Armstrong started his group in the 1930s and it's a reason for conjecture among former members as to whether he intended to be a cult leader or not. My own view is that he had most likely genuine motives at the start to make a difference but as the years went on and he became more and more powerful, he was distracted by his influence over others and by his notoriety. Also by the huge amounts of cash flowing into the cult from its often struggling members.

He felt that he was given a job to do by God himself and that he was chosen to alert the people of the Earth to what he saw as the coming wrath of God.

Older readers may remember *The Plain Truth*. This was a magazine published by the cult with a large circulation in the millions all over the world. To give it some credit, the publication was well respected and the articles were researched carefully for the most part. It was a news magazine but concentrated mostly on what was seen as proof that the times of trouble were close.

The cult also enjoyed a lot of air-play with its *The World Tomorrow* radio show and later, a TV program of the same name. The cult's magazine and radio program spread across the US and Canada during the 1940s and 50s then onto Europe and the UK as well.

British authorities didn't allow the program over radio on the mainland so the cult, not to be defeated, placed its message on pirate stations off the coast. The magazine and electronic media shows found their way to our nation as well, and it was through the radio program that my parents came into contact with the group. Later, my own dealings with WCG will be discussed in more detail and you will see how my life was badly disrupted by this former cult.

THE WORLDWIDE CHURCH OF GOD

For years, the modern-day "apostle", as Armstrong liked to be known, traveled all over the planet, bringing the group's message to many world leaders who actually granted him an audience, such was his charisma and influence. He did this in a private jet, all paid for by the cult members apparently limitless pockets of course.

Armstrong saw mainstream Christianity as being weak, wishy-washy and as lacking direction. He said that so-called Christianity focused too much on Christ himself rather than on the message he brought during his time on Earth. He strongly believed that the writings of the Old Testament were not just there for us to learn from but rather that the Old Covenant between God and Israel was still to be largely lived by even today.

Because of this view, the cult strongly adhered to a belief that the seventh day Sabbath should still be observed strictly. This in my view was one of the worst aspects of life within the sect.

Many people who were nurses, police officers, ambulance officers or in fact anyone who had a job which involved the likelihood of having to work on the Sabbath was forced to give them up if they wanted to become cult members.

FROM FEAR TO FREEDOM

In one case which I am aware of, a member was allowed to remain within the Queensland police service and was permitted to avoid Sabbath work by his employer, however, he was not eligible for normal promotion opportunities. In other cases, unemployment resulted, or people were obliged to take lower paid jobs even though they had fine qualifications, in order to avoid Sabbath work.

Work was not the only activity banned during the Sabbath. Sport, even as a spectator, shopping (except for essentials), volunteer work to help others and activities such as dancing or fishing were outlawed as well.

In my own case, during my teen years, I had an opportunity to try out for some disability sport because of vision impairment. I may have possibly been good enough to represent my state or my country as some of my non cult member friends did but due to the ban on Sabbath sport and even training, well I'll never know now.

WCG was typically cultish in many respects and believed that it and it alone was the "one true Church". It also believed that all other churches were deceived and of the devil. This led to a lack of trust towards it from most other religious groups and Worldwide was therefore on the fringes of Christian religion.

THE WORLDWIDE CHURCH OF GOD

WCG did not keep members physically isolated as some cults do. There were no gun-wielding guards, no barbed-wire fences and we lived in regular houses in regular cities and towns. There was though a strong effort by the cult to monopolize the time of its members, not only due to church services but also because of entertainment and sporting activities just for members and their families within the group.

Such activities may sound good on the surface and indeed, they did have a positive side, however they also served to restrict the time that we could spend with nonmember relatives and friends.

As well as the weekly Sabbath mentioned above, the cult practiced the annual Sabbaths covered in the Old Testament and such observances appeared positively weird to the uninitiated. For example, usually in March or April, the cult observed the "days of unleavened bread". Leavening agents such as baker's yeast were supposed to typify sin due to their ability to puff-up and members had to remove all such leavened products from homes, cars and work or school-bags etc. Try explaining that to a nonmember child friend at school and see how weird that seems? I tried to make sure my school mates didn't find out about any of these strange rituals because I didn't want to become a laughing-stock.

Another really strange observance was "the day of atonement". This was to typify the blame for all sin in the world being placed on the head of Satan. We celebrated this by going without all food and liquid for 24 hours.

My parents were very ill when they observed this for the first time and older children were also encouraged to do this as well. Going without food and water (fasting) was often encouraged as a tool of correction within the cult.

Also the cult saw food products from the pig or shell-fish as unclean and forbade the eating of them. During a sporting trip to Sydney with my school, bacon and eggs were served for breakfast one morning. Of course I tried to be a loyal cult child and didn't eat the bacon, I ate only the eggs and although they tasted great, it was hours before we ate again and I found it hard to compete on only half the food eaten by everyone else.

Such weird beliefs and behavior certainly did socially isolate WCG members from the rest of society. Even now at the age of 47, I don't have close relationships with extended family such as cousins which is at least in part due to the cult's social isolation for so many years.

THE WORLDWIDE CHURCH OF GOD

This is not an attempt to provide a concise history of Worldwide however it is an introduction to it and will at least give you some idea of what it's like to grow up in a cult. Such was the control the cult had over the thought processes of people within it that some former members just couldn't cope with life away from it after leaving. During a conversation with another former member and close friend, we came up with the names of 15 people whom we knew or knew of, who committed suicide because of being unable to cope with life outside the sect.

During the coming chapters as we discuss cults in general, further aspects of life in WCG will be described, as a way of placing you at the "coal-face", so to speak, of cultic life.

FROM FEAR TO FREEDOM

Chapter 2: What constitutes a cult?

It's all very well to talk about one cult or another but what is one? If you have never had any experience with cults, could you recognize a harmful one if you came across it?

Around the world there are many churches and most seek only to do good. Some bring help to people of all types regardless of their religious affiliations if any. These genuine organizations also provide a peaceful environment for their members to gather together and worship God according to their particular belief. Leaders of such churches try to point the way to God and do not seek to be elevated to a status which interferes with the congregation's view of God.

FROM FEAR TO FREEDOM

The gentle and patient guide, and the supporting behavior towards individual spiritual searches and journeys, rather than the overbearing doctrinaire controlling behavior, are the marks of difference between a genuine church and a controlling cult.

How unfortunate it would be then if a genuine church with no motives to bring harm and only good were to be mistakenly labeled as a religious cult. Equally, how sad it is that many controlling cults falsely present themselves as harmless churches and get away with it.

So how then do you tell if a particular group may be a damaging cult? If you have questions about a so-called church you are in or want to determine whether a group you are thinking of joining is out to help or harm you, then this question must be truthfully answered.

You will find a list here of characteristics which will help you in making this determination. This doesn't mean that all cults will be guilty of each and every factor, however it is a safe bet that a cult which could be destructive will exhibit the bulk of these problems. This list is general and not definitive - for a more technical explanation of how to spot a cult, please visit: www.factnet.org

WHAT CONSTITUTES A CULT?

Characteristics of a harmful cult:

- Usually headed by a strong and charismatic leader who may claim to have direct contact with God beyond that of anyone else, or may even claim to be God on Earth, Jesus, or speaking as some other famous religious leader reincarnated.

- The leader and those around him or her live a luxurious life-style while the regular member struggles in poverty due to financial demands placed on them by the cult.

- Cults frequently have a persecution complex, that is, they fear and teach their members to fear "the outside world".

- Cult messages often have a pre-occupation with fear of "the wrath to come". This is used to deliberately scare members and prospective members in order to gain their attention and make them susceptible to mind control.

- Ex-members are usually shunned and if a family member leaves the cult, it's not unusual for the cult to forbid contact between family remaining within it and "the one gone astray".

- Cults are often very secretive and try to stop religious services and other group activities from being viewed by "outsiders".

- A cult may condone or even encourage a member to break the law in the country where it operates believing that the group is subject to only the law of God.
- Members are often discouraged or forbidden from seeking medical aid even if they are very ill. This may be seen as a lack of faith.
- People within a cult are usually not permitted to read books or other literature not written by a leader, minister or which has not been approved by someone senior within the group. Or if other sources of information are not banned altogether, they may be strongly discouraged or scorned.
- Cults are frequently given to elitism, that is, they teach that being within the organization will make members special, set apart and blessed by God.
- Children within a cult are sometimes discouraged or banned from seeking a regular education as the group may view such schooling as "of the devil".

WHAT CONSTITUTES A CULT?

The word cult simply means a group devoted to a person or thing. You could have a superman or star-trek cult for example. These aren't likely to be destructive unless people really become obsessed. Hopefully the description above will make it easier to sort out destructive cults from those which are not.

It will be obvious then that spending a significant amount of time in a manipulative and controlling cult leads to major damage to anyone and rebuilding a life afterwards is a huge challenge. In the next chapter we will look at how cults do so much harm to people all over the world.

FROM FEAR TO FREEDOM

Chapter 3: How do cults cause so much harm?

Isn't religion supposed to be all about love, goodness, and fixing the problems humanity faces? How is it that an organization which has a religious basis can cause dreadful harm to the life of a member and in some cases grief to his or her family and friends?

A religious cult will most likely have a benign sounding name which will probably include the word God in one form or another, Jesus or other prominent biblical identities, perhaps the name of its founder or of a key belief of the group. This name will give no clue to what really goes on within it. By way of example, can you see anything nasty about the name Worldwide Church of God? Yet it was a group causing harm to people in dozens of countries around the globe.

Not all cults are considered as troublesome, even though persuasive techniques may be used. Arguments over whether a particular group is a harmful cult will always occur, however a detailed look at some typical damaging cult behavior will help you make this important determination for yourself. Even if you decide a particular group is not totally cult-like, you will be able to decide what kinds of traits and behaviours are unhealthy or undesirable, and avoid them.

To examine how such organizations are so destructive, let's look at the characteristics of a cult discussed in chapter two with more detail.

1. Usually headed by a strong and charismatic leader who may claim to have direct contact with God beyond that of anyone else or may even claim to be God on Earth, Jesus, or speaking as some other famous religious leader re-incarnated.

In the case of a cult which is small in size, and confined to a limited local area, the leader will have total control over the group's affairs. He or she will be aware of the lives of each member and will have control or at least a large amount of influence over them.

With large cults spread over a whole country or around the world as Worldwide was, the leader must appoint a trusted group of elders or ministers to exercise his or her will in each local area. These people will be out to impress their leader or those above them if a chain of command exists and may be even more authoritarian than the leader is.

This continued mind control robs individual members of their normal ability to think clearly and thought processes become distorted with the cult's views on all aspects of life. People in this situation lose ability to make major and sometimes even minor decisions.

Worldwide had an authoritarian chain of command as its structure of Government from the top down and this is the way it was supposed to work. At the top was God the Father then Jesus the son of God, arch-angels such as Michael and Gabriel, regular angels, and here on Earth, Armstrong as the modern-day apostle, followed by a number of ministers with the rank of Evangelist. After that came ministers with a rank of Pastor, preaching elders, local elders and deacons with regular members at the bottom of the heap completing the story.

Get the picture? The chain of command was clearly defined and it was easy then for the cult to say that God was in charge and backed up all decisions made here on this planet within the group.

Members were taught that a challenge to the authority of Armstrong or a minister was a challenge to God himself. Obedience through fear was the result and people who are frightened are easy to control. We were taught that if a decision made by a superior within WCG was wrong and even if we knew it, we must still obey as God would sort it out.

> 2. The leader and those around him or her live a luxurious life-style while the regular member struggles in poverty due to financial demands placed on them by the cult.

Cults often demand or trick members into giving over large sums of money on a regular basis. Sometimes cults will take-over completely the control of the financial affairs of members.

Of course this results in poverty for the average member and although the money is supposedly used to preach the Gospel or to bring help to the needy, most of it seems to find its way into benefiting the leader and those high in the governmental structure of the group.

Good old WCG was typically cultish here too and as already mentioned, Armstrong flew all over the world in a private jet fully funded by the hard working and loyal members. The justification for this was that he had so many world leaders to visit, it just wouldn't be practical to use commercial airliners. How many "ordinary" members had a fly in it? I didn't even see it.

The pay local ministers or the other officials within the group received wasn't discussed, however large and well-appointed homes were the order of the day for these people. Only members who were personal friends or who informed on others received invitations to visit such places.

During my life in the cult, I can't remember such an invitation for my parents and I to visit, yet some of our much needed cash contributed to this wealth.

The cult prided itself on not passing an offering plate around during weekly church, however this was a crafty disguise as the group received huge amounts of money due to its enforcement of a corruption of the Old Testament tithing system.

As well as this, so-called free-will offerings were taken up during the seemingly endless round of church services throughout the annual Sabbaths, briefly covered earlier. The offering would be preceded by a message from the podium consisting of emotional black-mail describing how the "Church" needed as much cash as we could give in order to do God's work in the short time we supposedly had left.

> 3. Cults frequently have a persecution complex, that is, they fear and teach their members to fear "the outside world".

This behavior leads to the member suspecting the motives of anyone not in the group and causes extreme distrust. It also brings about division in families where one person is a cult member and others within the family are not. In many cases, contact between the cult member and his or her family "outside" is forbidden. This lack of normal family interaction is of particular harm in the case of second or third generation cult members. It is a situation that will be covered in more detail later.

During Chapter 1, I briefly mentioned how family ties were damaged for me because of social isolation. WCG believed that it would be persecuted and as members, we all dreaded this and sometimes discussed whether we would have the strength to admit that we were church members if the police or other authorities came to the front door. We were taught that even trusted neighbours would probably turn on us one day.

See the fear and the distrust? Children have huge issues with this when brought up with it and nightmares disturbed my sleep from time to time.

> 4. Cult messages often have a pre-occupation with fear of "the wrath to come". This is used to deliberately scare members and prospective members in order to gain their attention and make them susceptible to mind control.

It is beyond the purpose of this book to cover a lengthy and technical explanation of what mind control actually is, however for more detail on the subject, again please visit www.factnet.org

Suffice it to say here that mind control is a way of convincing someone of adopting a belief system that he or she wouldn't have otherwise come across as his or her own. Sleep deprivation and constant repetition of religious messages may be used to hammer home the belief system into the member or new recruit of the group.

FROM FEAR TO FREEDOM

High-tech sound and lighting effects are likely to produce an altered state of consciousness in a significant number of people, making them highly susceptible to various teachings of religious cults. The aim of the preacher is to reduce the function of the left side of the brain of the listener. This is the analytical side and is the most likely to resist new or radical messages. The right side of the brain is the creative and artistic side and is more suggestible. Of course resistance is not what cults need in order to gain new recruits.

Some sects use various meditation techniques, chanting or even drugs to break down resistance and turn people into virtual sponges, willing to absorb all of the ideas and beliefs of the group.

Cults often like to stress the more frightening parts of the Bible such as the book of Revelation, using these writings to bring fear into the thinking of members and prospective recruits.

Then the preacher from the cult promises "deliverance" from these horrible events provided of course the fearful person obeys in full all the teachings of the group and comes to God through and only through the path of the particular organization.

HOW DO CULTS CAUSE SO MUCH HARM?

Armstrong held to the doctrine known as "British Israelism", that is, he believed that the people of the US, Canada, Britain, some from northwestern Europe, Australia, New Zealand and the whites of South Africa were descended from the so-called lost tribes of Israel.

He also believed that a time of terrible and unimaginable punishment was about to come upon the above-mentioned people because of what he saw as our departure from the ways of God. We in Worldwide were taught that the most horrible tortures you could ever dread would soon come to our country.

If you are a sensitive person then this paragraph might cause some difficulty for you. As a child, I clearly remember a message in church when a torture apparently used by Japanese troops during WW2 was detailed. The victim was forced to drink as much water as possible and is made to lie down on their back. Then he or she is jumped on and the stomach is destroyed.

Would you tell a story like that to your kids before bedtime? Children in WCG had no choice; we had to listen to stuff like that, no wonder about the nightmares. The thrust of the message was to indicate that such terrible events were to happen again and we would go through it too if we didn't obey the teachings of the sect.

> 5. Ex-members are usually shunned and if a family member leaves the cult, it's not unusual for the cult to forbid contact between family remaining within it and "the one gone astray".

Where someone has been a cult member for many years, he or she may have no friends or very few outside the group. When such a person leaves the cult or is ex-communicated (usually for disciplinary reasons) they are likely to experience extreme loneliness. This person will also experience major fear and probable depression as he or she is taught to think that it is impossible to please God unless they are a loyal and obedient member of the group. Also a person in such a position is not likely to seek help from a counsellor or other qualified people due to the distrust issue covered earlier. Feelings of isolation and desperation are common and as mentioned earlier, tragically in some cases suicide is seen as the only escape.

Due to the authority of local ministers, members could be easily ex-communicated from this group. Sometimes WCG members were just suspended for a temporary time. One reason for this was "fornication". For some reason, suspension was usually for a longer time if such sexual activity resulted in pregnancy. Of course this was to teach a lesson and as a deterrent to others. In the long-term though such practices just re-enforced the fear of the minister and did nothing to help anyone.

Ex-communication could also be permanent and a typical reason for this was if a member was caught with so-called dissident literature. This was produced sometimes by former members and I very clearly remember an incident where I played a major role in the removal of a fellow-member.

We were taught to inform on each other if we knew of another member reading and or passing such material around among the group. I knew of such a person and thought I was doing the right thing, pleasing God, I phoned the local minister at the time about this and within a few days, the man was put out from the sect. That was many years ago and I have no idea what happened to him as I haven't seen him since.

Now I have no pride at all in that action but it shows how loyal cult members will do almost anything.

6. Cults are often very secretive and try to stop religious services and other group activities from being viewed by "outsiders".

This makes it difficult if not impossible for non-members who are trying to help a family member or friend to leave such a group to do so. In extreme cases, even police or government welfare workers are prevented from gaining access to the group. In a high-profile case some years ago in the US, a shoot-out resulted between the Branch Davidian cult and the FBI. Unfortunately a large number of people died in the resulting fire as the authorities tried to gain access to the property owned by the group.

WCG members lived in ordinary houses as mentioned above and as far as I know, the group didn't prevent or try to prevent access to any members by authorities. The cult did though force new recruits to read an amount of literature which was supposed to prepare them for membership before they would be allowed to attend church services. Walking in off the street to check out a church service was not permitted.

I remember an incident where one of my aunts asked about coming to a church service out of interest and with some embarrassment, my parents had to tell her not to come. I don't think she could work out why and who could blame her?

Doors would be locked before the group observed the Passover – the most solemn and serious commemoration of the sect, describing the death of Christ.

7. A cult may condone or even encourage members to break the law in the country where it operates, believing that the group is subject to only the law of God.

As a cult leader is likely to believe that he or she and the "flock" are only subject to the law of God (however they see it), this will cause conflict between the member and the government of the country where he or she lives. It's a particular problem if the religion in question is not permitted or if freedom of assembly is not allowed. In Australia, voting in Federal, State and Local elections is compulsory. Over the years, at least two cults including WCG forbade their members from voting and it was necessary for each member to indicate that this happened due to religious reasons in order to avoid a fine.

My parents and I (when I reached voting age) dreaded the please explain letter from the Australian Electoral Commission asking why we didn't vote after one poll or another.

FROM FEAR TO FREEDOM

Mum is totally blind, dad is severely vision impaired as I am and so we would have to ask another cult member to fill out the form and then we returned them to the AEC.

WCG justified this behavior by saying that we were subject only to the Government of God and we shouldn't have any interest in the affairs of another government.

   8. Members are often discouraged or forbidden from seeking medical aid even if they are very ill. This may be seen as a lack of faith.

For example, in one situation which I am aware of in Worldwide, a lady was diagnosed with a small benign tumor. Surgery was recommended and would have been just minor. This lady felt that it would be a lack of faith to go ahead with the removal of the tumor due to the teachings of the cult and many years later, the growth was huge. The cult eventually modified some of its beliefs and the lady's tumor was removed but the operation was much more difficult than it should have been. Even more drastic medical situations are sometimes left untreated by obedient cult members and at times, unnecessary death may result.

HOW DO CULTS CAUSE SO MUCH HARM?

Another even better known cult has forbidden blood transfusions no matter how urgent the need, and children who receive one have sometimes been disowned by their parents. That particular cult now has a confusing set of rules on blood fractions. Every Australian state legislated against preventing children from receiving blood transfusions as a result of that group's teaching.

9. People within a cult are usually not permitted to read books or other literature not written by a leader, minister or which has not been approved by someone senior within the group. Or if other sources of information are not banned altogether, they may be strongly discouraged or scorned.

This increases the control of a cult over its members and information which is not approved may perhaps plant a seed of doubt in a member's mind, so therefore it is forbidden. Again, it's all about mind-control or a more modern term which is coercive persuasion. If brain-washing is successful enough, even cults which do not physically isolate members can succeed in stopping people from reading literature not approved because such a person in this case thinks, "God knows what I am doing".

FROM FEAR TO FREEDOM

As described above, the reading of such disapproved material was grounds for ex-communication from Worldwide and debate over the teachings of that cult was seen as sowing discord.

> 10. Cults are frequently given to elitism, that is, they teach that being within the organization will make members special, set apart and blessed by God.

Who doesn't like to feel special now and then? If you get a better price on a new TV or computer than a neighbour or friend, aren't you just a little pleased? Don't you feel at least a little special? Holiday resorts like to make their guests feel pampered and special as it is something most of us enjoy. It has a down side though in destructive religious cults. Cult leaders of course know all about how to play on this longing and do it very well.

This is dangerous for at least two reasons. Firstly, a cult member may feel that laws of the country where he or she lives do not apply to him or her as mentioned above. This view can lead to a superior or contemptuous attitude when dealing with police or other authorities. Secondly, cult members are often promised special blessings from God due to their obedience and feelings of disillusionment may result when these do not happen.

HOW DO CULTS CAUSE SO MUCH HARM?

We in WCG were sometimes described as the "little flock" and made to feel special "set apart" as God's people. We believed that we alone knew the course of Bible prophecy and how it would impact the planet and this country.

We were taught that we and only us would be taken to a "place of safety" to receive special protection from God himself, while the rest of humanity would endure the types of torture and death discussed briefly above, because of sins. The rest of humanity of course included family members and friends not in the sect and anyone who had been ex-communicated.

When I returned from school each day, my loving and devoted Mum would always be there to greet me. She would never, ever be out when I arrived home! One day though, Mum was out shopping with the next-door neighbour and I think the car broke down before I came home.

This was in the early 1970s when belief in this place of safety was still strong. I marched up to the front door as normal and Mum wasn't there. No mobile phones were at hand then so she couldn't tell me that she was running late due to her neighbour's car troubles. A gut-wrenching and horrible fear suddenly gripped me as I thought, have they gone? As a child of about the age of 9 or 10, I thought do I now have to face the "great tribulation" and "the day of the LORD" (time of God's punishment) alone?

Many years later, I told Mum and Dad about this, and they assured me that they wouldn't have gone without me, but children don't always think rationally and I will never forget the fear and feelings of isolation that day. Also parents were told to leave if the order came through from Armstrong regardless of their children, as God himself would look after them.

This place was supposed to probably be Petra, sometimes described as the ancient rose-red City of the Dead due to the number of burial chambers there and because of the colour of the local rock. It's located in Jordan and as time went on, the place of safety was discussed less and less and of course, the group was never taken anywhere, just another Armstrongism.

> 11. Children within a cult are sometimes discouraged or banned from seeking a regular education as the group may view such schooling as "of the devil".

Obviously children in this situation are at a major disadvantage particularly when they seek employment later. Even after leaving a cult, such contempt for and fear of education causes a person to struggle with normal life and the missed opportunities for a regular schooling may never be available again.

I must credit Armstrong with a strong belief in obtaining a good education and in fact, education is a law given great praise in his book "the 7 laws of success". Also the group had a well-respected learning institution with two campuses in the US and one in England called Ambassador College.

This strong belief was though somewhat undermined by his teaching that the education institutions of this world such as schools, colleges and universities were all part of Satan's system.

This view meant that parents including mine believed that children should only do what was necessary at school and nothing more, in order to minimize their exposure to the system of the devil. Also as briefly mentioned, we were of the view that "time was short" meaning that the wrath of God was about to descend on society. We were taught that any lost education would be more than made up in the Kingdom of God or at the place of safety.

FROM FEAR TO FREEDOM

If you have had no experience with a cult and are perhaps reading this book with the idea of helping a relative or friend in mind, then you will see just what damage being in such an organization does. Some counsellors do specialize in helping cult survivors reconstruct their lives but in my view, it is still a neglected area of counselling in Australia. Society needs to be aware of what cult survivors are up against and more resources need to be directed at the situation.

Most of us have some idea of how much harm domestic violence and other forms of abuse cause to survivors, yet even though thousands of people have been harmed by cults of many different types, the subject is still poorly understood here in this country and it seems that most politicians, at least from the major parties, are not willing to take a good hard look at the problem. Could it be that there are just not enough cult survivors to swing votes at the next election?

Chapter 4: Why would anyone join a cult?

As we have seen, religious cults may be very dangerous or even life-threatening. Why then would some people give part or full control of their lives over to such a group if it is going to hurt them?

It should be remembered by anyone reading this who has not been involved in a cult that leaders of such organizations are very persuasive. If they were not, then their groups would never get off the ground. Of course not only religious cult leaders are able to persuade, by way of example, Adolf Hitler dazzled the crowds with his powerful speeches and haven't we all heard of people being talked into something by a door-to-door sales person?

A cult leader though is particularly dangerous as he or she is likely to claim that they have the backing of the Lord himself. This adds a lot of weight with any God-fearing individual. A leader or other preacher from a religious sect may say to a member something like this, we may not know what you are doing but God does. As a result even if a member goes on a trip to some remote location such as the Australian outback (assuming it is allowed) obedience will be assured.

In the early 1990s, my then wife Joan and I went with a group of friends from the cult to Stradbroke Island east of Brisbane. We were there for three days camping and all had a good time. At that time, mobile phones were not common and my portable ham radio set was the only means of communication handy.

Even with this isolation, someone brought a tape recorder along so we could hear a taped sermon on the Sabbath. No one would have known if we didn't play it but we all felt that it would be wrong not too. See how members will obey even when not being observed?

We will divide cult members and new recruits into two groups; this is in order to better examine how people end up in cults in the first place and to more thoroughly understand the challenges faced by survivors as we rebuild our lives.

Firstly there are people who join such a sect as teenagers or during adulthood. We all are aware of our physical human needs such as the requirement to keep our bodies hydrated and the need for food, clothing and shelter. Most people have social needs as well and we enjoy the company of others through relationships and friendships.

For thousands of years, many human beings have also felt a need to connect spiritually with a God or a creator however they see such an entity. Beliefs in an after-life are widespread around the world and are not new. The Pharaohs of ancient Egypt were surrounded by many luxury goods in the tomb as it was believed that these would assist them on their journey to the next life after physical death.

Most religions teach that how we live here now on Earth will have a bearing on our ability to enjoy a good life in Heaven or what is seen as paradise. Many individuals satisfy this spiritual hunger by joining one of the world's major religions or perhaps by going along to a meditation group.

FROM FEAR TO FREEDOM

This gives the person concerned a sense of calmness and a feeling of being a part of a purpose larger than themselves.

There is sometimes a stage in a person's life when he or she actively searches for a belief system to cling to – an organization which will offer guidance, that sense of security and belonging. This may happen during young adulthood or even during the teen years as an individual builds the structure of his or her life, or perhaps as a result of disillusionment with established religion.

Such a search may be rewarding and ultimately satisfying, however those mounting such efforts are vulnerable if they come across a cult during this time. Also people from abusive backgrounds may be looking for a way of escape and may see a religious sect as a place where they can be guided, feel secure and protected. In this situation, he or she will suffer more abuse, perhaps worse than at home.

My parents' case shows how cults may take advantage of people trying to find the truth. Both were brought up in mainstream religion, but became turned off by what they saw as a lack of interest and empathy from the church nearby.

As luck would have it, at this time, while searching for something with more meaning, they

WHY WOULD ANYONE JOIN A CULT?

came across *The World Tomorrow* program on radio.

As mentioned, this was produced by WCG and was hosted at the time by Herbert Armstrong himself or by his son Garner-Ted. This happened in 1965 and after contacting the "Church" they were sent literature compulsory to the process of becoming a member.

Due to vision impairment, the material had to be read onto tape for Mum and Dad. Going through this entire process took about 3 years and my parents were baptized as WCG members in 1968. They then became what are known now as first generation cult members.

Cults tailor messages to the general public carefully and recruits are not aware of the true nature of the organization until well into the journey toward membership. By the time they become aware of what is happening, it may be too late for him or her to avoid hurt if the brain-washing process is successful.

The second group in our study is those who join by default in childhood or even as babies, as a result of a decision by parents or guardians to become cult members. Those of us in this position had no choice in the matter and face huge challenges when learning to live outside the cult where we may have spent years or decades. We are known as second generation members and if a cult lasts long enough, third or even fourth generation members are possible.

A typical second generation cult member's case is that of my own. When I was at the tender age of three, my parents came into contact with WCG. Is a child of that age going to recognize a cult? Is he or she going to say, "No, I don't think that sounds right?" Certainly not, especially in the 1960s, a child wouldn't dare even if he or she had a bad feeling about it.

I have no real pre-cult memories and 31 years is a huge slice of a person's life. I was very fortunately though able to make life-long friends at school and as these children were not cult members, I did have some normal childhood interaction.

As I grew up, family activities such as Christmas parties, birthday parties or Easter celebrations weren't permitted due to the beliefs of WCG.

I observed Christmas for the first time in 1996 at the age of 34 and it felt very, very strange indeed. Christmas was banned because observances on the 25th of December can be traced back to a time long before Christ and Armstrong felt that this was enough of a reason to not only forbid it but to call it a feast of Satan.

He believed that Christ was born much earlier in the year, probably around September as the shepherds wouldn't have been out in the December snow with the sheep. This may be correct but it's hard to justify the hatred with which the cult viewed this celebration.

The celebrations mentioned above are frequently a time when families get together in countries like Australia and WCG's refusal to allow them only led to damage of family ties. In my situation and for many other second or third generation cult members, family ties with people outside the cult are never properly formed at all.

People in this group have been exposed to cult messages from day one and do not have many or any pre-cult memories to look back to. We are often badly harmed even more than the first group, as our formative years are partly or fully spent in the sect.

Both groups have issues in common and also difficulties which apply to one group more than the other. Later, we will look at the challenges faced by both lots of cult survivors as we rebuild our lives.

Chapter 5: A bumpy ride through Worldwide

Now that we have had a good general look at what destructive cults are all about, let's have a detailed examination of one particular cultic upbringing, namely that of my own - so we can see the cultic hurt and isolation in all its glory. This shows the years of emotional pain faced by second generation cult members during childhood and how it follows on into adulthood.

In this chapter, I have chosen deliberately to take advantage of my unusual view of growing up in WCG. That is, from the point of view of a severely vision impaired person. I have not been to the US and so have not had the pleasure of

FROM FEAR TO FREEDOM

visiting the headquarters of the group when it existed. From my viewpoint though, I am very well placed to expose the hypocrisy which existed with WCG for many decades. After all, if an organization can't show love to its members who have a disability then could it really call itself Christian?

In most cases, not everything about being in a cult is bad and that was also my experience, so I will try to describe positive events which I experienced within the organization from time to time.

My earliest memories of WCG are of being told to play quietly by my parents, while they listened to many many hours of church material read for them on tape before being permitted to attend services. I didn't take long to associate church with boredom even though I hadn't yet been to a service.

Not long after my sixth birthday, my parents were approved by the local minister to attend church. I soon found that spending a minimum of two hours each week during services was very, very dull indeed. This was just the time of the service and didn't include time before and after when we were supposed to fellowship.

A BUMPY RIDE THROUGH WORLDWIDE

During these meetings, most children of a young age were permitted to sit on a mat on the floor and draw, read, look at pictures or colour-in. Of course with hardly any sight, none of this was possible for me.

I already had a good imagination and could visualize just about anything. I soon learned to do this in order to avoid being bored out of my head during tens of thousands of hours spent in church. I would fly planes, play in bands, go fishing, run, swim and do it all in my mind. It may sound crazy but it was my only escape.

Strangely in later years after learning how to meditate, I've found this ability very helpful. In my older childhood when I was supposed to actually listen to the preacher, I would still sometimes sit there while off somewhere in my head and then feel guilty about it later. I guess I had a faraway look on my face then but my dear parents couldn't see it, so they couldn't correct what they were not aware of.

The first services I attended were at the South Brisbane Library Hall (long since demolished) and then the Brisbane Church as we were known moved to the Salisbury High School Hall in the southern suburbs. This was a large school hall for our city in those days and one horrible memory jumps very clearly to mind from that time.

The group was very, very strongly in favor of corporal punishment for children and messages about so-called child rearing mainly revolved around this subject. Both the men's and women's toilets were about 5 or more metres behind the last row of seats within the building. It was necessary to open two heavy spring-loaded timber doors in order to access those toilets. Even with such barriers, it was still very easy to hear child after child being clobbered for some misdemeanor or other.

Fathers and sometimes mothers would take children to the toilet to punish them and the screams would start long before the above mentioned rooms were reached. This early screaming only resulted in more severe beatings. Such sounds rapidly brought me back from any imaginary trip I was enjoying and now I can still hear those as I write. Fear was a constant companion for many children then. Although I feared the prophecies of the Bible, I must say my parents didn't treat me that way.

Sometimes people not in the cult would remark on how well behaved children were within the group, however what they weren't aware of is that the crap would be bashed out of such children if they even came close to playing up.

During the so called Annual Sabbaths, we were subjected to at least four hours of services and again, this didn't include fellowship time before and after. The format would be a two hour meeting in the morning, then lunch for about two hours and another lot of church for at least the same length of time in the afternoon.

Those days were exhausting especially for a child who hated all of it. My life in WCG during childhood was very, very lonely. I didn't have any real friends and just simply sat there waiting to go home. I sometimes saw other children playing as they went past but didn't have enough vision and was far too shy to go with them.

As well as this, I was mostly ignored as if I didn't exist by other children my own age. Many years later, one or two of those children (then grown up) came to me and said that they would have liked to have played with me but didn't know how to interact with a vision impaired boy. What a pity their parents didn't try to teach them how and what a pity WCG didn't make a better effort to love everybody according to their preaching.

FROM FEAR TO FREEDOM

The main issue I had to deal with as I grew up was constantly being different. In the cult I was different due to my disability and even among my mates at school who were also vision impaired or blind, I was different because of the cult. I was the square peg only finding round holes.

During childhood it was fairly easy to escape as mentioned above from the boredom and loneliness. As I reached my teens though the problem only became worse. By then, I actually began to understand most of the preaching and had formed the view that even with all of the painful rejection, Worldwide was really the true church. In other words, all of that brain-washing worked on me.

I did really listen some of the time at that age and that's when the fear of "not making it" really set in. I think it was in the mid-1970s that a youth group was formed within the church called YOU, Youth Opportunities United. As I was without friends at that time within WCG, I had no interest in it at all.

Sometime later, to my absolute horror, Armstrong in his wisdom made it compulsory for all young people aged between 13 and 18 to be members of YOU. I hated it with a passion and would sit there at the YOU meetings being ignored and waiting again to go home. Many of the activities

organized for the youth-group were very good and included: shooting, archery, horse-riding, rock-climbing etc.
With 5% vision though, I couldn't take part.

I very, very much anticipated my 18th birthday, not so I could vote or drink alcohol but rather so I could get out of that damned YOU.

In the early 1980s, a Dutch family moved to Brisbane and began coming to church. All three sons of the family were friendly toward me even with my disability and their oldest son and I began to form a fairly strong friendship. From that point, my social life within WCG improved slowly but surely. This being the case though, I didn't at any time feel like a completely accepted part of the sect.

During my late teens and on into my 20s, my parents regularly invited a group of members over for dinner. These evenings became a social highlight for me and I would look forward to them eagerly. They were never officially a part of cult activities though.

The last Annual Sabbaths of the year, the *Feast of Tabernacles* and the *Last Great Day* were meant to commemorate the setting-up of God's Kingdom on Earth. As such, the cult actually enjoyed itself for seven days. A 10th of a member's income would be put aside for this and many good times were had. My parents tried to ensure that I had fun too and bought toys for me in my early childhood. Later, I was able to enjoy fishing, tours and a number of other activities such as flying in a light aircraft, hot-air ballooning and bungee jumping.

We would have enjoyed these "feasts" as they were called in any case, but the experience was more intense because of the huge contrast with the regular grind of daily life in the organization. The exciting activities described helped a little to make up for even more time spent in church during the "feast".

When I was in the cult, two church services were held every day during this feast up until about the early 80s. Before my parents and I joined, some days, there were 3 services per day. That's a minimum of 6 hours of church each day. It's hard to keep awake for all of that and as mentioned elsewhere, sleep deprivation is very cultish as it breaks down resistance.

I was baptized as a member of WCG in my own right in 1982 and yes, I actually believed in it. I thought it was the only true church as we were taught repeatedly, even though I couldn't understand why I had no friends while growing up in it.

During my youth, I would blame myself if I was ignored by my fellow teenagers as that is what we were taught to do. We were constantly told "if you want friends, you must show yourself friendly". This of course is true and works in normal society but not in WCG or at least not for someone with vision impairment. The confusing part for me though was this, why did I have some wonderful friends at school but not in the "Church"?

At that time, my parents reluctantly allowed me to spend an occasional weekend away with a friend from school and his family. Even more reluctantly Mum and Dad allowed me to attend his Baptist Church youth group with him and the cult was never told about this. To my absolute amazement, his youth group accepted and welcomed him even though he also was vision impaired.

How could this be? How could one of Satan's churches, as we were taught all other religions were, actually show more love to people with a disability than WCG? I struggled with this question for many years and didn't really answer it until discovering that WCG was just another horrible deceptive cult.

FROM FEAR TO FREEDOM

My school friends are still with me as mates today, and showing myself friendly certainly worked with them for which I will be forever grateful.

The cult had its own public speaking club set up in a similar way to Toastmasters. This was called *Spokesman's Club* and was only open to baptized men. Membership of this wasn't compulsory, however it was highly recommended by the ministry within WCG as a way men could grow as a man, leader, husband and father.

We usually referred to it as "club" and it sort of became an unofficial rite of passage among men within the cult – a way to sort out the men from the boys. I was baptized at age 20 and many years before that, I knew that I would attempt club one day and dreaded it for a long time.

The concepts within Spokesman's Club were sound and it did help a lot of men including yours truly grow and learn to control shyness. As you will read though, many men used speech evaluations to verbally rip other men apart and in many cases, the minister in charge (known as the director) let it go on.

Some men found what was learned at club helped a lot during regular life, particularly when they were called upon to give speeches or presentations at work. In my own case, I'm a member of a number of clubs and associations now and have found a public speaking ability very useful at times. Spokesman Club was mainly responsible for this.

I remember the gut-wrenching fear on the night I gave my first speech. This first talk in the 12 speech program was known as the ice-breaker and was designed to let the speaker introduce himself. There were 30 men in club when I joined but of course, I was the only one with vision impairment.

Many years before being baptized while still a teenager, I went along to club as a guest with a member. I enjoyed listening until I heard what I thought was a great speech being absolutely torn apart. The speaker was verbally torn asunder as well and the evaluator/humiliator actually laughed at this poor man. Equally horrible, some other men at club that night joined in the merriment and the director didn't intervene at all.

I was hoping to avoid such a fate and although my time in club was very tough, I was treated better than that. I heard older men say that club when I was a member was hard but not as bad as years earlier.

FROM FEAR TO FREEDOM

For almost all my time in club, I deliberately avoided any mention of my vision impairment in case the other men thought I was looking for an easier ride through the course. With one speech though I decided to speak about life as a person with vision impairment. The title of it was *breaking down the barriers* and it was meant to show the realities of life for people with this disability on a daily basis.

One aspect of this was the fact that eye-contact is often very difficult if not impossible for us. In my own case, my left eye looks in a somewhat different direction to the right and there's nothing I can do about it. The speech was well received and was passed by the director. It was the next time I spoke though when I realized that for the most-part, I was wasting my time. After the end of my following speech, the evaluator criticized me for wait for it, *"not having enough eye-contact with the audience"*.

Can you believe that? After all that work to present vision impairment during the speech before, this ignorant idiot obviously didn't listen to a word of it and yes, he was there during the *breaking down the barriers* speech.

I then realized that many men were too busy looking for fault with the speaker rather than listening to what he actually said. I am convinced that many real valuable learning opportunities were missed because of that.

We were taught never to back-chat the evaluator but on that night as he mentioned my poor eye-contact, I wanted to do more than back-chat the drip.

Strangely enough, although club was very hard, I didn't hate it like I did with YOU. I think it was because even with vision impairment, I was able to measure-up and to pass all 12 speeches on the first try. As I proved to have some public speaking ability, I gained a bit of respect and wasn't treated like a retarded idiot. This meant a lot to me but I had to earn it the hard way.

The director decided whether or not a man passed his speech assignment and had the power to fail him. Many men were failed and some repeatedly, meaning that they had to try several times to obtain a pass on one assignment or another before moving on. Being a cult, of course no chance to appeal against repeated failures existed.

Even with the respect I earned, I still didn't really make any new friends at club and the men who were friendly towards me there were blokes I already knew.

I was absolutely and deeply disgusted by the treatment meted out to another club member who also has a disability. He is a stroke victim and as a result, has an impaired memory. This meant that he had a heavy reliance on notes. We were taught to use only key-word notes to jog the memory.

As mentioned, this man didn't have much ability to remember and yet almost every time he spoke, some dipstick would harshly criticize him during the evaluation for an overuse of notes. Where was the brotherly love there? Where was the Christianity?

At that time in WCG, the dating scene was heavily controlled by the local minister. This meant that it was almost impossible for a young man and a young lady to develop a friendship without the minister sticking his nose in.

There were 2 extremes, people who wanted to date had to hardly see each other or be counselling for marriage. No time was allowed to actually develop a friendship first. The average time of a typical engagement in WCG during the 80s when I was involved in the dating scene was about 8 to 12 weeks.

A BUMPY RIDE THROUGH WORLDWIDE

No wonder then a lot of marriages later went on to fail including my own. I am not certain why this hurry was the case, the only explanation I have is that WCG was so paranoid about people fornicating that they wanted to make it "legal" as fast as possible.

Local ministers enjoyed a lot of power over the everyday lives of WCG members and the following example will show just how this was wielded. It also shows just how much fear particularly second generation members had of ministers and how obedient we were.

Not long after Joan and I were married within the sect, we were visited by the minister who was the second in charge in our church area during that time. Our spare bedroom was untidy as it was being used as a "junk room".

We closed the door before this man visited so he wouldn't be offended by it however during a trip to the toilet, without our permission, he opened the door and took a long look inside.

After returning from the toilet, he proceeded to give us a 15 minute lecture on how Adam was charged with keeping the Garden of Eden clean and that also meant we must fix the spare room immediately.

Of course being totally obedient cult members, we didn't even think of challenging such a directive and took it all right on the chin. If such a thing happened in my life now, I would give him 10 seconds to get off the property before calling the police. I hope this means that I have progressed as a free-thinking adult.

As I look back now on my cultic upbringing, I know that the time was tough but being able to use my experiences to help others puts some purpose back into my life.

Although I am not a psychologist or counsellor, I have a good general knowledge of how cults work and feel safe in the knowledge that I should be able to spot a religious, commercial or political cult with relative ease.

Chapter 6:
Preparing to leave

It is impossible for me to be familiar with individual circumstances, therefore the contents of this chapter are written in a general sense and as a guide only.

Why do some people leave an organization where they may have spent years, decades or perhaps in which they grew up?

If a religious cult is extreme enough, it may self-destruct in a very dramatic and tragic way. This has occurred in at least two cases and a large number of innocent people died as a result. The first well-known case was in Guyana and the second in Waco, Texas.

The persecution complex mentioned above plays a major part in such a situation, with leaders of

FROM FEAR TO FREEDOM

these sects becoming more and more paranoid about what they perceive as likely outside intervention in the fate of their groups. They feel that the will of God can only be carried out if the group is completely separated from the possibility of outside interference as they see it. The death of the entire cult is of course a way of guaranteeing that ultimate separation and in a twisted way, it is felt that being a martyr to the cause will greatly please God.

Obviously anyone who survives such an experience will be greatly traumatized and would be strongly advised to seek counselling as soon as possible, from a very experienced and highly qualified counsellor able to assist cult survivors to rebuild their lives.

Thankfully not all cults go out in such a terrible way. Most religious sects do not survive the death or incapacitation of their leader. In such a situation, those just below the cult leader in authority are likely to start disagreeing over what path the group should take into the future.

In-fighting and a power struggle will be the case and the group will fall apart. In these cases, splinter groups will probably form and these will disagree with the parent organization and even with each other. Ex-members of the main cult will sometimes go among the splinter groups searching for "the faith once delivered".

In 1986, the highly revered leader of WCG passed on. The cult was rocked by this event as it was felt that he and his son would be the two witnesses discussed in the biblical writings of Revelation, although I don't think this was ever official doctrine.

Before his death, Armstrong appointed a successor, Joseph W. Tkach. This man was in my view far more honest than Armstrong ever was. He set about exposing many of the false teachings of the group, even though he knew he would cause huge upheaval and enormous damage to the organisation's income.

Many people such as me, already with doubts, followed up on Tkach's new ideas and the other members with questions began to learn to actually research without fear of ex-communication.

Some though disagreed greatly with his new views and clung strongly to Armstrong's old original teachings. Many splinter groups broke away from WCG and these were led by former leaders under Armstrong within the parent cult. Each of these men wanted to be in charge and as usual when a cult falls apart, they disagreed with each other and with WCG itself.

Major confusion, anger, hatred and bitterness were the result with WCG, as is usual with imploding cults. This makes the recovery process for survivors even more difficult and time consuming. In the situation where a person is or was in a cult which falls apart around them, (hopefully without tragedy) they have no group left and have to face life outside, like it or not.

Others will sometimes struggle with questioning thoughts in their minds as I did (usually in secret) having doubts about the sect and its teachings or behavior. Such people may finally develop the courage to break away from the cult and if you are one, then congratulations. You have made a brave and rewarding decision with a major prize as the result. That is, gaining or regaining control of your life.

You may be the first to leave your particular cult but if it is a large one then chances are you are not. Cults normally teach that your life will turn bad and that you will face huge trials if you ever leave. Of course this is to deliberately cause fear and to retain membership. You are likely to hear that God will be angry with you and that he will directly punish you for disobedience. This is the ultimate fear card that any cult can play and carries enormous weight.

Please know though that over the years, thousands of people have left cults all over the world including myself and to my knowledge, none have been struck or zapped by God. This is not to trivialize very real fears suffered by many former or current cult members, including the writer. Ask yourself though, would a loving God strike me down because I no longer am a member of one group or another?

You will only face problems common to all on this planet except of course for those passed onto you by the cult itself. After the right counselling and with time and some work on your part, you can go on to rebuild your life. By all means contact other former members of your group, but beware of bitterness. The other ex-members are used to being in an unhealthy group, and may have bad behavior habits. Your former co-religionists who are still in the group are trapped in a controlling system – feel compassion and forgiveness towards them, rather than bitterness and vengefulness.

The cult stole your past; please do not allow it to rob you of your future as well. If you know of

FROM FEAR TO FREEDOM

former members of your group who have left and are successfully moving on, then if possible, you may wish to make contact with them as they will know exactly what faces you upon leaving. Hopefully they will be willing and able to assist you. Trust is the issue here though, as I have heard of actual cult members masquerading as counsellors in order to collect information on straying followers.

Be careful of telling current members of any plans to leave, as they may not see things the way you do and might inform against you to gain favor with superiors within the group. Also such people will probably consider it as their duty to try and bring you "back to the fold". If possible, select a counsellor with at least a bachelor degree or masters – you are unlikely to find good quality counsellors with a diploma only. Some of these diplomas are handed out with about six weeks of training.

My decision to leave Worldwide came as a result of increasing doubts over the teachings of the sect and due to what I saw as a major conflict between the messages preached from the podium and the actual life within it.

As I grew up, I believed wholeheartedly that the cult's beliefs were totally true and correct and it's a little scary to think of just how much I would have put on the line to support that view. This didn't mean though that I was a good little boy, and I struggled much of the time inwardly with a secret rebellion. I sometimes deliberately misbehaved at school in order to prove to my mates that I wasn't religious and was the same as they were, even though this wasn't true.

WCG didn't officially discriminate against anyone, however it was given to understand that those from a supposedly Israelitish background were superior to people from Asia and to those with black skins – the so-called "gentiles". It was often preached that Jesus went to the cross without blemish and although WCG also didn't discriminate against people with disabilities, unofficially, anyone with a physical difference was treated as if we weren't quite as good as the rest of the membership.

This included people in wheelchairs, those who were over-weight, anyone hearing impaired and of course, as I have only about 5% vision, I had a blemish too. My parents had quite a number of friends in their age-group even with their vision impairment, however the young people in the sect seemed even more unwilling than their older counterparts to try and accept a vision impaired youth.

FROM FEAR TO FREEDOM

This meant of course that I was lonely within the cult as we discussed in Chapter 5, even though sometimes I was supposedly part of a congregation of hundreds. It also led to my beginning to question in later years how a group which constantly preached "we are family" could treat people this way.

This was the major reason for my doubts mentioned above and under the leadership of Tkach those doubts grew and grew with less and less fear. Joan (my wife at the time) also had major questions, but to her the process of walking out of the cult was easier. This is not meant to indicate that Joan didn't suffer within the cult as she most certainly did, but she seemed to have an inner knowing that we wouldn't suffer the anger of God due to leaving WCG.

From anecdotal evidence, men often found it harder than women to leave WCG and often had more trouble coming to grips with fear and anger issues afterwards. Eventually Joan and I left the cult in March of 1996 and I faced two major different emotions afterwards.

Firstly, I felt a huge relief that we could actually have a whole weekend without having to spend half of it keeping the Sabbath. Secondly, I felt fear of the decision we had made and kept waiting for

PREPARING TO LEAVE

God to "get me". I constantly waited for my life to turn bad after leaving as we were always taught would happen to anyone who left the sect.

I didn't know at the time just how much my thought processes were scrambled by the cultic teachings of WCG and as a result, didn't know how much damage was done to me. Also at the time, the concept of a cult survivor support group hadn't even occurred to me and I probably wouldn't have believed that I needed one in any case.

Later counselling indicated at least in part how the cult had influenced me and had filled me with fear and a very low self-esteem. Cult survivor support groups are filled with people just like us, that is, those who have spent years or even decades in religious cults and who are now rebuilding their lives.

Official support organizations are the safest way to go, especially if an experienced cult survivor counsellor heads the group.

If you have the freedom to use the internet then it is a very good place to search for cult survivor information and as well as the website already mentioned, a reference list of cult survivor support groups appears in this book. If all else fails, type cult survivor support groups into your search engine. You may wish to specify which country you want to search for more locally based groups. Such support organizations will have experienced cult survivor counsellors among their members or will be able to refer you to one. If your cult is or was large, then chances are that a former member is in a support group in your area.

If you need to talk with police or other authorities in order to receive protection or to report dangerous cult activities, then a cult survivor support organization will be able to help you. It will most likely be able to provide someone to accompany you while dealing with authorities if needed. You don't have to face these issues on your own – that is what support groups are all about.

Leaving a religious group which has controlled your life for many years or decades is an enormous challenge, but the rewards are even larger. Your life is yours and yours alone, you are the one who should decide on its future course, not some greedy and manipulative cult leader.

Chapter 7: Life after the cult

Welcome to the rest of your life – it is yours and no one else's to control. You have started on the course toward building or rebuilding your future and will soon be able to take your place in society as a strong and confident human being.

Before this can happen though, it is important to realize that this is not an immediate process. A lot of hard work and determination on your part is needed and first you must be certain just how much harm you have experienced from the cult.

This will depend on the teachings and behavior of the sect, your length of time as a member and your individual reaction to the experiences. Many

FROM FEAR TO FREEDOM

former members of harmful cults suffer from ongoing anger and fear issues as a result of what they have been through. Anger at the damage caused by the cult and the lost opportunities in life due to restrictions placed on them by the beliefs of the group. Also fear of the future brought about by many hours of brain-washing during cultic church services or other ceremonies.

Ex-members will try to stop fearing that "God is going to get us" but this fear has probably been so engrained that it may take some years to escape from. These problems are described in more detail in the next chapter.

As well as the issues mentioned above, you may feel very lonely and isolated as a former cult member if your friends and possibly family are still in the group. Contact is likely not to be allowed between you and them as mentioned earlier.

Here again is a vitally important place for your cult survivor support group. Members of it know how it feels and will be able to help you deal with the rollercoaster ride of emotions you are likely to experience.

If other members have left the group along with you then there is nothing wrong with trying to help each other, after all, you are dealing with the same issues. You will be able to support each other into the future as you all gain or regain the freedom Australians so greatly value.

There is a trap here though for the unwary, such a group of ex cult members can go from being an unofficial support group to being one which breeds anger, hatred and a desire for vengeance. While such feelings are totally understandable, they will not help any of us gain the lives we want and have a basic human right to enjoy. Your group in such cases may degenerate into a hate and anger session and the opportunity for mutual support is lost. While it is helpful to talk through your experiences, preoccupation with what was done to you within the cult only causes anger and magnifies harm already caused.

Be aware that many people who leave groups think it will be really easy to bring their cult down, and in fact most of the cults around the world, by simply setting up a website and phoning a politician. Please understand the relationship between governments and cults is a tough one. No western government will tread hard on the freedom of religion. And governments have been struggling with religion since the Roman Empire (which lost).

FROM FEAR TO FREEDOM

As I look back at my own case in order to write about it, I see that I experienced some years of anger. That problem is largely behind me now but I still struggle almost every day with the fear issue.

I don't know how my life would have turned out if I hadn't been in WCG for all of those years and continued time wasting thinking about it isn't at all helpful. Even if I live to say the age of 80, 31 years of cultic experience is still an enormous part of a human life. If I look at my case from purely a physical human point of view, then the bulk of my life so far has been not much more than a waste of time.

Let me share though how I have come to terms with what happened to me and how I find the strength to get out of bed each day. Over the years I have often talked with former Worldwide members like me and have seen some trying to deal with the troubles discussed above. Some have not succeeded and are no longer with us.

It is not my intention to preach any particular belief system here, however I will briefly cover what helped me find a strong sense of purpose in what's left of my life. I will never again join any religious organization, however I have become a very spiritual person and look forward to participating in a meditation group every week. I have an unshakable view that there is certainly life after this human existence.

Looking at my former cultic life from this view, what's 31 years when compared with eternity? Not much is it and in the meantime, if I can use my own experiences to help others as I am trying to do here, then it all seems worthwhile after all.

You are free now but what will you do with your freedom? It is extremely important to handle your new free life with great maturity. As stated right at the start of this book, some people become members of other cults or rejoin the one they left because they find that the new freedom is just too daunting. It is easier to let someone else tell them what to do again. Or they take up alcohol or drugs after leaving a harmful cult. This occurs when people do not seek support and are not fully aware of how much damage the sect has actually caused.

Alcohol and other drugs may give short-term relief and may help you temporarily to forget the cultic life you were a part of, but in the long-term they will only add to your troubles. Also such drugs make it much harder to think clearly and therefore harder to recover.

FROM FEAR TO FREEDOM

Especially in the case of second generation members, prolonged abuse of one sort or another within the cult will actually damage a person's ability to become fully mature. In this situation, a member may leave a cult at say the age of 35 but only have the maturity of say about an 18 or 20 year old. This can result in such a person wanting to try all of the things he or she "missed out on" during all of those years in the religious group.

This could mean going to night-clubs, seeing what it is like to get drunk, or having a puff of that funny cigarette. Such experiences alone may not do much harm but without maturity, alcohol addiction or a downward spiral of drug-dependence may follow. Obviously then, the new freedom so highly treasured could be very destructive, perhaps even more than the cult itself. This is the reason then why your freedom, while being precious, must be used very, very carefully. Perhaps it is a little like water, that is, you can swim in it, go fishing or sailing on it and have a great time with it but you can also drown in it.

In my case, I had no idea at all how to use all of this sudden new freedom outside the cult and soon found out what it felt like to get rotten drunk for the first time. WCG didn't ban alcohol in any way and in fact, alcoholism was a problem within the sect. It did of course preach that drunkenness was sinful though and I had never been seriously intoxicated until after leaving the cult.

I even tried one of those funny smelling and illegal cigarettes and was not well as a result for three days. I must have taken a much larger drag than was necessary and therefore received a huge dose.

Friends and family members may try to help you at this time in your life and accept that they are doing their best here. If though they have never been in a cult or some other brain-washing organization, then they will have no real idea what you are dealing with. Try to be understanding as they attempt to make life better for you but do not expect them to totally identify with your issues.

My friends who never had anything to do with cults have always been there for me and I have had one or two interesting chats with my extended family members about life in WCG, however they can't quite understand how strange life was for my parents and I.

People have gone on to rebuild their lives after dreadful experiences such as concentration camps, gang-rape and other horrible events. You will as well if you take the support that is out there and

FROM FEAR TO FREEDOM

be determined enough to take control of your future.

Try to avoid the victim tag as a preoccupation with that status is not helpful and leads to self-pity. You are a survivor, not a victim and it is time to show yourself and those around you what you can really do now that you are gaining charge of your destiny. The cult experience will not be the defining centrality of your existence going forward – it will be only a part of your life. Your goals, your spirituality and your future will define you.

Chapter 8: Moving on

We hear terms a lot now days such as, "I've moved on now" or "I'm over it". How do we achieve that when we have been through such a terrible experience because of a cult?

Many religious cults of a destructive nature will teach members that they must put as much as possible memories of their lives before they joined the group out from their minds, suggesting that such times were evil and did not please God. They will try to instill the belief that only the present time and the future within the sect are important and that members should feel shame regarding time spent in life before "being called".

Once again, let's look at our two groups of former cult members. If you joined a harmful sect in the teen years or during adulthood, then you will hopefully have clear recollection of what we may call pre-cult memories.

Although you may have suffered abuse at home before coming into contact with the religious group, hopefully you still have some positive memories of life before the cult. Did you go out to the movies with friends? What about learning to dance, catch fish or that first date?

You may have lost contact with family and friends due to physical or social isolation caused by the cult but may be able to rebuild such relationships and make a new start. The less time you have been in the cult then the easier this should be.

Family and friends who have had nothing to do with cults will not have much understanding of your situation and may ask difficult questions. For example, where have you been? Or why did you change so much? They may even criticize and judge you and if this happens, gently but firmly remind them that they have not been in a cult and that they don't know what it's like.

Being honest with relatives and friends and telling them what happened to you will give them at least some idea of your situation and of the task you now face, that is, rebuilding your life. Also this puts the blame for your issues where it belongs, with the cult, not with you.

MOVING ON

When you feel ready, mention to former friends that you want to rebuild friendships and that you wish to rejoin social circles but will need time to readjust. You may also like to refer those among your family and friends who are interested to websites or books about cults and the harm they cause. This will inform them about what you face now in your new life and helps them to gain a deeper understanding of your situation. It is better to be known as a cult survivor rather than to be thought of as weird or crazy. Remember you have been taken advantage of by very manipulative and deceptive people and this does not mean you are stupid or gullible. Your effort to find a belief system to cling to has been abused and your enquiring mind has been led astray.

Questions you may ask yourself such as: How could I have been so stupid? Or how did I go along with that rubbish are normal as you sort your mind out, but they are not helpful. Questions like these will only add to your already low self-esteem issues. Remember – it was not primarily your fault that you joined the group. Mainly you joined because of the skill of the recruiters, or because you were born there or taken there by your parents.

FROM FEAR TO FREEDOM

Why did you join the cult in the first place? Were you caught in an abusive situation at home, school or in some other environment? It may have been an unusually stressful time in your life, such as early university, or when you had experienced some kind of relationship breakdown. That is not you now. When talking with your counsellor, it would be beneficial to you if you bring this out in order to deal with these issues.

When you have been able to come to grips with difficulties from your past, then the feeling that you need protection and shelter will not be a part of your life. As some people seek the apparent comfort and guidance offered by cults, developing emotional strength, self-esteem and a strong sense of identity will help you avoid being drawn into another harmful sect.

Second generation ex-cult members will have no or very few pre-cult or non-cult memories and will have spent most if not all of their lives in the group, as we have discussed. Such people will most likely have not enjoyed things taken for granted by most children or young adults who grow up in Australia.

Young people growing up in Worldwide were denied normal enjoyment in this country such as Christmas and birthdays as previously covered. Before becoming full members a water baptism

ceremony was required and after such, dating between baptized and unbaptized people even within the group wasn't permitted. Of course dating between people in the cult and anyone outside wasn't allowed either.
Some more extreme groups don't allow the use of computers, TV or radio as well.

Second generation cult survivors are not relearning how to live a "normal" life (however you see it) rather, it is all new to us.

As mentioned above, two of the most difficult and damaging issues any cult survivor will have to deal with are anger and fear.

Firstly, there is anger, due to the deception and all of those lost years. This feeling is totally normal in a human being, however, it is important to realize that prolonged anger will not achieve anything. It will not change the cult (if it still exists) and it will not repair your life. Instead, prolonged anger will destroy you and actually allows the cult to continue harming you, even though you may have left its membership years ago. Usually, you will not be able to "get even", or destroy the cult with a campaign or legal action.

FROM FEAR TO FREEDOM

How then do we deal with this destructive emotion? Believe it or not, we must come to the point where we can forgive. Are you thinking, *"but that just allows the cult leaders to get away with it"*? If you still believe in God, then leave it to him to sort it out. If not, then the universe and karma will deal with these deceptive people and you do not have to wreck the rest of your life trying to do it.

I have actually come across stories about victims of violent crimes including rape who have come to the point of forgiveness. On occasions, such people have even met their attackers and have forgiven them.

Forgiveness is in fact all about us, that is, it is letting go of these harmful memories which otherwise continue to cause so much harm, and it is about releasing the negative emotions such as anger and fear which go with them.

Research indicates that most violent criminals such as murderers and rapists are victims themselves. Often these people endure many horrible events during childhood. Research also shows that cult leaders' issues are transmitted into the cult. In other words, the issues of the leader become the issues of the cult he or she starts.

MOVING ON

Cult leaders are also most likely victims as well, growing up with abuse of one sort or another. Perhaps feeling insecure or as if no one really takes them seriously. It's only natural then that when he or she has an opportunity to influence and even control others, they will take it. Does this make their abuses somehow justified? Certainly not, however perhaps knowing that one cult leader or another also is a victim just might make the process of forgiveness a little easier.

I have often felt major frustration because of all of that lost time in the cult, due to some missed opportunities for different experiences. I must come to a point though where I can forgive if I am ever to enjoy peace of mind. Otherwise the former cult continues to rule my life even though I left it 14 years ago at the time of writing.

In my case though, forgiveness would have been easier if WCG was ever really serious about coming to terms in full with the harm its teachings inflicted on members and former members. In that event it should have used some of the remaining cash given by us to fund counselling so we could be assisted to move on. This would have shown that the sect was actually willing to reach out to the people it hurt so badly. This should have been a high priority before it tried to attract new recruits. Instead, property owned by the sect and of course paid for by the long-suffering members was sold-off and the cash didn't benefit any of us.

About 9 or 10 years ago, Joan and I wrote a letter to the then head of the cult in Australia describing the harm we endured within the group and we asked for a response from him. To our great surprise, we did actually receive one; he admitted that people may have been hurt within the "Church" as he saw it. He indicated that in his view, the ministers had the best of intentions at the time and that no harm was deliberately caused to anyone.

We were pleased that he replied but his letter was very carefully worded and in our view, it was written to head-off the possibility of litigation. If so, then he obviously felt more strongly about the future of the cult as it was at the time than about trying to help two former members move on from emotional trauma caused by the teachings of the group.

This of course isn't a surprise at all and although no longer married, Joan and I have maintained a good friendship. We have both reached the point where we can see that no matter what the view of former cult ministers is, we will move on by forgiving. This may not help the leaders of WCG as it was but it releases us and allows new lives to be built. That's what the forgiveness process is all about.

Recently I noticed an ad from a lawyer on a cult survivor website. I won't quote from it but the thrust of it was that the firm would litigate against cults and former cults in order to recover lost money duped out of ex-members. Do this if you want but such a case might cost you a fortune and may take years. Even if you win, how much sleep will you lose and is your case based on anger? If so, you may get some money back but what about the gray hair and the upset stomach?

In a similar way, fear is usually a normal part of the life of any current or previous religious cult member. While it has a place in our lives and is designed to help us avoid danger, if it is prolonged then like anger it causes major damage. Fear can be a cause of depression and may also harm one's physical health.

In the short-term, most cult survivor support groups will be able to help you with the acute part of starting or restarting your life away from the cult. That is when you need to deal with issues such as where you will live or severe emotional trauma. Please take this support as trying to rebuild on your own is much, much harder.

FROM FEAR TO FREEDOM

During the long-term as you move away from the urgent part of your rebuilding journey, you are likely to notice that cult survivor support groups tend to look at the issue of rebuilding from two different viewpoints – neither of which is wrong.

Some support groups will provide you with a religious way of dealing with your cultic past. This is fine if you have preserved a faith in God and these groups will actually be able to counter the teachings of cults from the Bible. If you choose to take this road then such support groups will help you rediscover religion as they see it. That is, without destructive cultic control.

If this path is the one you wish to journey down then you will be able to rebuild your faith in God through mainstream religion hopefully without any fear.

Other support groups which assist cult survivors look at the issue from a secular viewpoint. Many former members of cults choose not to have anything to do with religion at all. Some people wish to put their lives back together without anything that even looks like religion - totally non-religious help is provided by the second type of support groups described here.

MOVING ON

If you wish to remain a member of a group to gain assistance in the long-term then you will need to decide which direction suits you. Then any cult survivor support group should be willing to describe their way of helping with recovery, so you may make your choice.

If you take one path to recovery and other former members of your cult or from other cults take another, then please respect those decisions and avoid judging each other. Harsh judging is cultish and that is what we are moving away from.

As the process of starting or restarting a normal and wonderful life in this great country continues, then spend time making friends who have not had anything to do with cults. This will broaden your outlook and helps you to move away from having too many thoughts about the past and all its horrors.

I am fortunate here in that I have a good number of friends from many walks of life. This has helped me to move away from my cultic experiences and helps me to switch the focus to the present and even the future, rather than on what WCG was about.

FROM FEAR TO FREEDOM

As you move forward and as part of this wonderful freedom then you may find more spare time than you ever had before. The cult is not around to rule any longer and to monopolize your time. Why not take up a new sport or hobby? This assists with making friends and helps you use your time constructively.

Look at that secondary education you missed out on or check out a college or university course – perhaps it is not too late to gain at least some of those lost opportunities after all.

People with a healthy self-image are much harder to control therefore cults love to smash the normal feelings of self-worth we all should have. Often they confuse self-esteem with arrogance, and humility with self-hatred. A major part of moving on then is to set about rebuilding a healthy sense of self-worth. When you feel good about yourself then you won't look so much for acceptance from others and this removes a major vulnerability to cultic recruitment.

Part of my own life rebuilding process was to undertake a self-esteem development course and I also enjoyed learning about computers at TAFE. This helped me see that my life could still have some meaning and could be of use to others as well as to me.

Chapter 9: Helping the helper

This section of our study into the damage caused by destructive cults is written with those who are trying to help friends or family members harmed by such religious sects in mind.

Let me say a big thankyou for your efforts if you are trying to lend assistance to such a person as he or she rebuilds a damaged life. If you have never had an experience with a cult or in some other situation where you have been controlled or brainwashed then hopefully you have learned from websites, books on cults or perhaps from this material just what sort of harm is caused by such situations.

FROM FEAR TO FREEDOM

I also hope you will see how the rational thought processes of a cult survivor are likely to be badly distorted by the belief systems of the particular group, especially when fear is involved as we've just discussed.

It is a fact of human existence that we need to experience something ourselves in order to totally and completely identify with it. I hate the death and destruction caused by war, yet such conflicts interest me strongly and because of this I delve into information on various battles when I can.

As a result of this interest, I have heard many interviews over the years with war veterans. Typically, they will comment along the lines that the experience was so horrible that you can't fully understand it unless you were actually there.

I have a good imagination and can visualize almost anything, including what it might be like to face the terrors of battle. The important word here though is "might", as I have never been there. Therefore I can't totally know what it's really like.

Victims of floods, cyclones, fires and violent crimes are likely to make similar statements as well. A counsellor or psychologist will have a degree from a college or university and will be able to explain from an academic viewpoint what a cult survivor is dealing with. Also they will state how he or she should be feeling at any given time but even with such understanding, they won't know how it actually "feels" to have spent many years in a cult unless they have spent time in such a group. This is why in my view, the best counsellors are the ones who have been there just like us.

So how do you help a friend or relative in a cult? If this person is an adult and is happy to remain within the group, then you may not be able to do a lot about it in this country. You can try pointing out problems that you see within the sect and you can ask if he or she is really and truly happy and satisfied with no doubts or fears.

You could attempt to show this person any material which you have found that indicates the particular group might be harmful, however be very careful here. If your friend or family member chooses not to listen or look at your material then continued badgering from you may drive him or her further into the group. Remember they have probably been told not to read or listen to anything critical of the religion.

You might ask if the person is totally in charge of their lives and whether he or she feels any guilt if some directive from the sect isn't followed? Does he or she feel guilty if a meeting of the group is missed? Avoid strong criticism of the cult as this often results in the member becoming defensive.

Showing interest in the happenings within the religion can encourage the member to talk, but be careful here too as you don't want to be seen as a possible new recruit. Please avoid using the word cult or sect when talking about his or her group as these almost always have a negative slant.

Try to make sure your concerns about one group or another are based on a genuine belief that such a religious sect is definitely destructive and not on a personal dislike or grudge against it. If the particular cult is fairly large and has been around for a while then facts on it should be available and the internet is a good place to start now days.

The key to dealing with family or friends who are in the group is remember to build bridges, not burn them. Express your doubts carefully, in a manner which may encourage them to question. Telling them they are brainwashed or deceived is likely to be counterproductive. Encouraging them to increase their level of analytical thinking, rather than just accepting what the cult tells them may cause questions to arise.

HELPING THE HELPER

The ultimate hope here is that such questioning will lead to a point where your cult member loved one or friend is able to see the deception going on for themselves. In that case, they may eventually grow enough courage to "become a walk away". Meaning that they leave the cult and your help would then have been invaluable.

If you are a parent of someone who is not yet of adult age and he or she is falling into the grip of a cult which you believe is causing harm, then contact a large cult survivor support group. This issue is likely to be complicated and will probably involve the court system. It is beyond the scope of general material such as this. Similarly, if your marriage has broken down and your former partner is taking children into the group or keeping them there, the first step is to ensure a "parenting plan" is agreed, which should be done through an experienced family solicitor.

If your friend or family member remains within the group then please, always be willing to accept contact when or if it is possible. Sometimes people leave cults after many years so never give up hope.

If your relative or friend comes to you while leaving or attempting to leave the group, be ready to lend immediate help if requested and please DON'T JUDGE. Also I ask you as a cult survivor myself to avoid the following comments or questions:

- Why did you walk away from your family?
- How could you believe all that rubbish?
- Well now you're out of that stupid church, you'll have to get a job.
- I hope you don't bring any of that crazy religion around here.
- What's the problem? Can't you just get on with life now?
- You've left that mad cult so now come to church with me.

Such questions or statements are totally understandable but they show a complete ignorance of the situation facing your relative or friend and also they are very judgmental. Remember cult members are almost always exposed to judging on possibly a daily basis. If a former cult member is unfortunate enough to run into the types of comments above, that could drive them right back into the sect where he or she may still feel safe.

If your friend needs urgent help with accommodation for example, then please assist, however handing over large amounts of money is not a good idea. He or she may not be able to handle it and if contact still occurs between this person and the cult, some or all of it may end up going to the sect.

Be there to guide and gently advise if asked, but try to help your loved one to make his or her own decisions rather than deciding for them. The cult would have made many decisions for its members and when learning to live outside a destructive sect, we need to reach the ability to arrive at important decisions ourselves. Of course this takes time but with proper counselling, it becomes easier.

May I ask you to imagine for a moment that something long held to be a fact of history didn't really happen? For example if you saw proof that man never really went to walk on the moon at all. Rather, if it could be proven to you that it was just a trick of Hollywood, how would you feel? Wouldn't you feel lied to and cheated? You would be likely to think something like this, well if that's all make-believe, then what else is also?

On a personal level, if you suddenly found out in adulthood or as a teenager that your parents were not really your parents at all, rather that you had been adopted, how would you feel? This comes as

FROM FEAR TO FREEDOM

a shock to an adoptee and is similar to a cult
survivor finding out one way or another that most
or all of the teachings which we believed totally to
be true are not. Our whole world is turned totally
upside-down.

Feelings of anger, betrayal, and a strong
unwillingness to trust anyone are common. The
cult survivor reasons, if I've been deceived once
so badly, then who can I trust ever again?

Not only will future belief in religion or the ability
to ever have a faith in a belief system be damaged
but trust in partners within relationships is likely
to be harmed as well.

Feelings of being like a small ship on a large
ocean without a rudder are common as the cult
survivor comes to grips with the reality of being
outside. Some people report a "floating feeling"
from time to time and they may appear spaced-out
at times. Apparently words, phrases or certain
situations experienced can rapidly remind them of
times within the cult. An altered state of
consciousness may briefly occur like that
deliberately caused within the group. Fortunately
the condition normally clears up after some
months in most people. In a small number of cases
though it may last much longer and if this is so for
you, please seek counselling or recommend that
your loved one does do so as soon as possible.

HELPING THE HELPER

This is what your loved one is dealing with and you are sure to need patience as you bring help.

Try looking at it this way, someone who has been in the armed forces for many years will probably have some difficulty readjusting to civilian life where there are no orders to follow.

In a similar way, a person who is released from prison after spending many years there will also have large challenges learning to live outside the institution where everything was organized for them. You guessed it: it's likely to be very similar for someone coming out of a religious cult.

The freedom as we have seen is great, but it can be terrifying as well as it forces the cult survivor to take charge of their own destiny – something foreign to someone in a controlling sect or relationship.

Your loved one's view of the sect in which they were a member is likely to be strongly influenced by the way he or she came out from it. If they walked out of their own accord, then their view is probably going to largely be one of distrust, contempt and fear.

FROM FEAR TO FREEDOM

On the other hand, if he or she was kicked out for some reason, then they may view themselves as the reason for the issue. That is, they are likely to think, "There's nothing wrong with the group, it's all my fault", or, "I just am not good enough to measure-up."

In this case, your loved one or friend might think of the sect as something they should still really belong to and might view the cult with sympathy and even love. Remember the cult was family to us and particularly if a member is booted out, he or she feels grief as you would if losing your place within a family.

Over the years during many conversations with other former members of WCG, I have found that most of us have struggled along with very little help at all in rebuilding our lives. A close friend of mine found that his wife didn't understand his issues even though she spent many years in the sect herself. Her experiences were very different to his largely because her mother protected her from the worst aspects of the group and so this lady felt that her husband was exaggerating his plight.

My friend on the other hand was exposed to the very worst of WCG and was repeatedly beaten by his father in the name of discipline. This man felt at the time that he couldn't even turn to his wife for understanding and help in dealing with cultic issues.

The point I wish to make here is that if you are able to lend assistance to a cult survivor, then it can make a real difference if you go about it properly.

In the long-term, lending help to a cult survivor may be a satisfying and rewarding experience. You will learn a lot about an ugly side of human life, that is, the damage caused when one person or a group of people decide to deceive and control others. If your loved one is successful in rebuilding a shattered life, it will be like watching a beautiful flower opening. When that happens, you will know that your help has contributed to the rescuing and setting free of another human with the right to choose their own destiny.

FROM FEAR TO FREEDOM

Chapter 10: A note to Worldwide

I must start this chapter with a word of congratulations to the current leadership of WCG or as your organization seems to be known now in the US, Grace Communion International (GCI). This is because you actually acknowledge the cultic past of your church. Also I see on your website that you openly state that the organisation's founder Armstrong was plainly wrong in many of his teachings.

As well as this, I see that GCI has been accepted into the broader evangelical religious movement in the United States and although I will never be a member again, I view this as a positive. I don't identify as a Christian nowadays, however it's

FROM FEAR TO FREEDOM

most pleasing to me that your group no longer teaches that all other religions are deceived and are of the devil.

Of course such teachings are very cultic and these new views appear to mean that you have definitely left your cultic roots back in the past where they belong. I feel safe in saying that a child growing up in GCI would have a good chance at a normal life and wouldn't go through the sorts of abuse described elsewhere here.

You have probably gone further than most if not all other former cults in facing your past and this can't have been an easy process so I say, very well done to all of you.

My view of your church as a former member of 31 years isn't entirely rosy though and let me say why this is so. I left the former WCG in 1996 and in the same year your leader issued a letter of apology for the harm that your earlier teachings caused to current and former members.

This letter was sent to some members as far as I know but only to those within the US Is it too late to remind you that your former name was <u>Worldwide </u>Church of God? Meaning that in my view, it should have gone out to members everywhere, not just in America. I understand that the letter was read out in church here in Brisbane but that didn't reach out to those like me who had already left the group and we didn't all have the internet back then. People all over the world were greatly harmed by the teachings of the former cult and some went onto suicide here as well as in the US.

I knew some of these people personally and went through Spokesman Club with one. A letter of apology was a start but in Australia at least, that's where it stopped. Did you actually put any serious thought into how former members were really doing in the hugely difficult task of rebuilding shattered lives?

I have recently become aware of an organization called ORM which means Office of Reconciliation Ministry. This seems to be an arm of GCI and is dealing with huge issues such as racism and religious conflict. It works in places such as the US and Northern Ireland and appears to be doing a great job of healing many wounds. I am delighted about this and wish such an organization operated here in this country.

ORM has apparently helped a number of former WCG members in the painful process of facing their future after years or decades of cultic abuse and I would have given a lot to enjoy such support in my life some years ago.

A letter of apology is easy to write. I could write one even without much education but where were you when those who experienced on-going fear and nightmares here in Australia fought so hard to move on? The letter of apology is in my view heart-felt, very genuine and I imagine it caused Joe Tkach Junior (your leader as I write) some pain as he confronted the past of WCG as well as he could, but where was help of a practical nature for thousands of people trying to rebuild our lives?

How can a Christian church as you like to regard yourselves just ride off into the sunset so to speak leaving former members to their own devices? I don't see much Christian love in that, do you? This was and still is the reality of life for former members in this country.

As the ORM seems to be doing such a great job in reaching out to former members in helping some to rebuild and heal, then why is it so small? Shouldn't it be a matter of urgency to expand it as fast as possible to encourage such healing for ex-members all over the world?

If WCG damaged lives in any particular country then in my view, the ORM should also be working in that same country in an effort to reach out and heal. Do I hear you say we can't afford it? Well put simply, if many years ago you could afford to damage and hurt people all over the planet, then you must try very, very hard now to undo that hurt whenever you can.

Instead, you have the gall to actually try and attract new members who are most likely largely unaware of the real and dreadful damage your religion caused. Are you so afraid of litigation that you felt it necessary to dodge and weave your way around the worst aspects of WCG's past?

Joe Tkach Junior's letter addresses very clearly and without reservation the hurt caused by the scriptural and spiritual errors of the former WCG but I find no mention of emotional and financial damage cause for decades by the group. Also I failed to find a mention of the suicides among former members. I only hope that this isn't because he is unaware of them or because he can't bring himself to confront the dreadful truth. That is, that WCG and Armstrong's fear-filled teachings actually drove some people over the edge.

I am delighted to say that my efforts to rebuild my own life have largely succeeded however if this were not the case, would I be able to visit a service or go to your office in Queensland and ask for help? There is no ORM here so I would most likely receive a lecture from the Bible and be told about forgiveness. Or I might simply be told, we're not like that anymore. That of course is all true but if I needed cash for example and could actually prove that I was a former member, would I be given any?

WCG was happy to take hundreds of millions of dollars over the years from people all over the globe but where are you now if some of us need a little help? I needed counselling some years ago to get on with my life and the cost of it was very minimal because it was organized by the good old Salvation Army. How does it feel to know that another church had to come to the rescue of one of your former members? Shame on you.

As is obvious here, I respect your efforts to come to terms with your past but would have respected you a lot more if those efforts actually benefited those of us who were at the coalface of life in your organization here in Australia. Instead, I admire the progress you have made but view you as largely weak and lacking guts.

In order to offer practical help, why didn't Tkach cover the existence and value of cult survivor support groups? This would have pointed the way forward to people as we started the process of life rebuilding. See what I mean? Practical help was not dealt with at any time especially here in this country.

As you move forward, please, please don't forget the lessons of the past. Will you allow another leader like Armstrong to take control of your church and become a cult again? I feel that this is most unlikely however it is at least possible in theory. Fanaticism in any form is dangerous so please be sure to keep your teachings balanced and continue to maintain the new and much needed cooperation with other churches.

It's probably a bit too late now to seriously reach out to former members as most of us have rebuilt our lives in one way or another even in countries where ORM doesn't exist. But then you have the internet these days and sites such as Facebook. These can be used or even your own site to see if any assistance can be offered to ex-members – think about it.

During my time in your group, I personally saw a lot of harm which was done to not only me but to other members as well. Try this for example, in one case I am aware of, a local man in Queensland was married to an "unconverted" woman. She didn't like his involvement in your former cult and made him decide between it and his marriage to her. Of course, as you would expect, he decided in the cult's favor. To make matters worse, he and this lady had a daughter and this man's marriage fell apart. To my knowledge, there has been very little contact if any between him and his daughter since.

These lives were badly damaged by your former teachings and did Tkach's letter of apology truly sincerely as it was meant really help?

If that situation doesn't move you then perhaps this one will? In another case I am aware of again locally, a married couple experienced major problems in their relationship. They separated and wanted to divorce. WCG at that time (during the early 70s) didn't recognize divorce and the couple were forced back together. Of course the relationship again foundered and they had to go through the pain of another separation a second time. Some years later, the man shot himself.

The point I am making here is that the letter of apology is a great start but do any of you really and completely understand the true and dreadful harm Armstrong's teachings actually did? If so then please realize that a letter of apology won't do much at all except act as window-dressing.

A NOTE TO WORLDWIDE

I understand that you are a Christian church and in Tkach's letter he quotes a scripture from Philippians. This I suppose will reach out to those who have maintained their Christian faith but may I mention to you that not all former members have done so. Some of us have been turned-off that faith forever by your former belief system. If you ever try and reach out to members or former members again, please try not to quote the bible at us. After all, Armstrong did that many thousands of times as he rammed teachings down our throats which tore our lives apart.

I wish you only the best as you move on and also wish to say here that I have forgiven the former cult and as much as possible, the individual ministers who were responsible for the harm and disadvantage which I experienced within Worldwide.

My focus now is on helping other former cult members of your group and hopefully a lot of others as well. Out of a spirit of honesty, why not make sure that your current membership is informed about what really happened in WCG from its beginning until Armstrong passed on? Perhaps asking some former members to present talks at some of your services would be a good start. This is not to forever dwell in the past but

FROM FEAR TO FREEDOM

rather to understand it fully and then move on determined never to allow it to happen again. This would also show just how much real progress you have made.

I will also try to encourage other former members of the religion to forgive as much as possible. As we know, it's the best and really the only way for all to move on.

Chapter 11: Reaching out to the splinter groups

The leadership change from Armstrong to Joseph W Tkach Snr was smooth and orderly. It seemed that for a while at least, all would continue as before in WCG after Armstrong's passing. It didn't take Tkach long though to start to question a few and later many of WCG's views.

As the years passed, more and more of the doctrines which were central to the former cult were brought into question and changed. Some ministers under Tkach were supportive and even carried out further research on the teachings of the group in order to strive for greater Biblical accuracy. Such men presented their findings to Tkach Snr without fear of being fired as they would have been under Armstrong if they disagreed with him.

Tkach felt that he couldn't just standby while members of WCG labored under old and heavy cultic views that could be proven wrong. Tkach had spent time many years earlier in the US military and had the guts to take on a challenge. He felt strongly that the church should continue to exist but that it should be reformed from a fringe-dwelling cult to a main-stream Christian religion.

Unfortunately though, many ministers under Tkach's authority didn't agree with him at all. These men had the view that Armstrong's teachings were the only ones that should be held to and that Tkach was deserting the faith once delivered. As a result, a large number of such men left the parent group over a period of about 10 years and set up their own organizations.

They poached large numbers of WCG members off with them and these groups disagreed strongly with WCG as it was and also couldn't agree with each other either. Oh where was the Christianity here? At one time, well over 100 different groups existed and some break-aways broke from the

REACHING OUT TO THE SPLINTER GROUPS

break-aways, are you confused now? I don't blame you if you are!

I would like to address the leaders of such splinter groups here if I may. Why oh why are you stuck in the past? Why is it that you can't seem to see the results of Armstrong's teachings when such are so obvious for all to examine? The accounts here in this book are absolutely true and these are from the grass-roots so to speak showing the life damaging consequences of that former cult leader's views in action. Why are so many of you desperate to repeat the mistakes made and now acknowledged by Worldwide?

Are you so totally blinded by your own attempts to cling to your power over others and to the cash dragged out of your hard-working members that you have lost any normal human empathy and compassion? Do you somehow think that it will be different this time? If so, you are deluded and more importantly, the people who are members of your cults will be hurt as I was in WCG.

Children growing up in your groups are going to suffer the same sort of abuses detailed here and do you really think that's what God wants? Further generations of people with wrecked lives will

FROM FEAR TO FREEDOM

come out of your organizations and I can guarantee it, how? Because Armstrong was just another cult leader and if you follow him then that's what you all are as well.

I only hope that one day all of you will stop hiding from the obvious truth and eventually that you can apologize for your cultic abuses as WCG has tried to do – the sooner the better.

If I may address those people who are caught-up as members of your splinter groups by your very successful fear-dependent deception? Let me say this, please, please take some time to research what actually happened in Worldwide. Not just here in this book but also have a look at Wikipedia as it's all there for your information.

Oh yes that's right, the cult won't allow you to do that will it? Well that's because it's just that, yet another nasty fear-filled so-called Bible-based Christian cult scared of what you will really find out about it and about Armstrong as well.

Have a real good look at the results of prolonged exposure to the belief system created by Herbert Armstrong. See the years of fear and the millions of dollars dragged out of the pockets of WCG's members. If you are in a group which is trying to hang on to Armstrong's teachings then it's happening to you as well.

REACHING OUT TO THE SPLINTER GROUPS

If WCG was the only true church as we were taught many hundreds of times then why did it have to change so much? Could you really still believe that all other churches are set up by Satan as Armstrong taught? Can't you see how totally cultic that is?

Will your children thank you for bashing them regularly, as parents were taught to do under Armstrong, when they grow up? Do you think that they might run away from you as fast as they can when they reach adulthood as they did after leaving WCG in many cases? That's highly likely because there's nothing new about Armstrong's views. They are old news and have been tried before only to be found severely at fault.

Please see Armstrong as he was, that is yet another cult leader with a message of fear, racism and domination. As a person with 31 years of experience of Armstrong's cultic belief system, I plead with you to get out of any organization using such views while you still can.

Church is something you are supposed to enjoy and benefit from, not something you should fear. Look at the past and learn from it, don't repeat it.

FROM FEAR TO FREEDOM

Conclusion

As I sit at the computer thinking of just how to finish the book which I have written as an effort to help my fellow cult survivors, a number of thoughts come to mind. Have a good hard look at modern society and you will see that it's not all bad.

Humankind has made some amazing progress toward a better life for all and let's have a brief look at some positives. Although domestic violence and child abuse still tragically happen, these subjects are openly discussed nowadays. Of course this doesn't solve the problem but it means that we don't bury our heads in the sand on the issue any more. If we communicate about an issue then surely that's a start toward dealing with it.

FROM FEAR TO FREEDOM

Even other creatures with whom we share this planet are benefiting from our new attitude of enlightenment. For example, most nations of the world no longer hunt whales and subject those amazing animals to a cruel and unnecessary death. Most people at least in our Western society now believe that such hunting is a thing of horror and should never have happened. That has to be progress doesn't it?

People with disabilities still face some tough times as I know all too well however issues such as discrimination are being dealt with by Governments at all levels and also by the private sector. Society as a whole is more likely to view people with disabilities as useful members rather than shutting us away as might have happened some decades ago.

I am a frequent rail commuter here in Brisbane and often see people in wheelchairs traveling with ease on and off of trains. This for the most-part wasn't possible even 20 or 30 years ago as many stations weren't wheelchair accessible and the trains weren't either.

Although I believe that the damage which religious cults do is still not well understood by the majority of people here in Australia, it's also true that more help is available now for us than would have been around say 20 years ago or more. So then, even we cult survivors are able to benefit from this progress in human thinking.

Unfortunately though it's not all good news. Even though World War II ended many decades ago, we still see that humankind thinks that international conflicts can sometimes be solved by military means.

Also if we look at the subject of deforestation, we see that we are making very little if any real progress at all. So it's a mixed bag then and sometimes people look at these ills of human society with a dream of making a real difference. What's wrong with that then? Well nothing unless such a person becomes corrupt and uses his talents of leadership to influence others to the point where he or she has undue control over them.

We might all have ideas of how we would like to change the world but if we ram those ideas down the throats of people looking for that strong leader then that can rapidly become cultic. We must change the world through cooperation not domination!

Also if we find a person with a powerful and charismatic personality having a strong message, and a group of people willing to listen and follow plus a place to meet then another cult is likely to join the thousands already reported all over the planet. In my experience I have seen even how something as innocuous as a meditation group has the potential to turn cultic. This may happen when one strong-willed individual has too much influence and when the others within the group are too willing to submit.

The message here is this: we must always remember that as adults, we and we alone are in charge of our minds and what goes into them. Trust your own intuition – that gut-feeling, if something seems wrong, then it just might be.

As you progress along your own path toward recovery from whatever cultic experiences you have been through, why not try writing a story on it? As I write, I'm finding the experience of doing so is helping me heal as well as helping others I hope. Even if you don't publish it, you might be surprised about just how much interest your family and friends show in your story and it's a way they will learn more about you and about cults in general.

In this way, a positive can come from your particular cultic journey no matter how horrible it may have been. Do I hear you say, but no one would be interested? Or I don't have a degree and

CONCLUSION

have no idea how to write anything? Well all of that also applies to me but even now I'm surprised by the interest shown in my story from family and friends – so go on, give it a go.

May I leave you with this final thought: recovery is surely about healing through forgiveness, not about vengeance or getting even.

FROM FEAR TO FREEDOM

Appendix

Reference list of cult survivor help groups and counselling organizations.

Cult information service.
This is a Brisbane-based cult survivor support group located in the Western Suburbs.
Telephone: (07) 38785212 or:
www.cultinfo.org.au

CIFS Cult information and family support.

This cult survivor and family support group operates from Sydney and Brisbane helping people all over Australia. Go to:
www.cifs.org.au
CIFS NSW: info@cifs.org.au
Ph: 0423-332-766
CIFS
GPO Box 1690
Sydney NSW 2001

CIFS QLD: infoqld@cifs.org.au

FROM FEAR TO FREEDOM

Ph: 0413-082-344
CIFS
PO Box 4002
St Lucia Sth Qld 4067

Concerned Christian Growth Ministries.

This organization offers Christian-based support for people leaving cults through its lookout service and is based in Western Australia.

Contact Options:
www.ccgm.org.au
50 Carcoola Street (Cnr. Carcoola Court), Nollamara,
WESTERN AUSTRALIA 6061
Tel: 618-(08) 9344 2200
Fax: 618-(08) 9344 4226
e-mail: info@lookout.org.au

Lifeline
Although this organization assists people all over the country with many issues, its 24 hour telephone counselling service would be a good place to start for crisis help. Also Lifeline offers face to face counselling by appointment if needed and low-cost assistance may be arranged.

Ph: 131114 or: www.lifeline.org.au

Salvation Army

We've all heard of it and this well-respected church appears to match its actions with its message, that is, it offers assistance to people in need everywhere just like Lifeline.

Salvo careline: 1300363622
www.salvationarmy.org.au

Beyond Blue

The National Depression Initiative, is dedicated to providing help to people suffering depression and as that illness is often part of a cult survivor's lot, it's well worth a look.

www.beyondblue.org.au
or Ph: 1300224636.

Manufactured by Amazon.ca
Bolton, ON

32966075R00077